... the

Caged

Bird

Sings

          and

The

Heart

of a

Woman   Maya Angelou

Selected from

I Know
Why the
Caged
Bird
Sings

and

The
Heart
of a
Woman

Maya Angelou

Additional material
Copyright © 1989
New Readers Press
U.S. Publishing Division of Laubach Literacy International
Box 131, Syracuse, New York 13210-0131

Printed in the United States of America

10   9   8   7   6   5

First printing: January 1989

ISBN 0-929631-04-8

The words "Writers' Voices" are a trademark of
New Readers Press

Cover designed by Paul Davis Studio

Acknowledgments

We gratefully acknowledge the generous support of the following foundations and corporations that made the publication of WRITERS' VOICES and NEW WRITERS' VOICES possible: The Booth Ferris Foundation; The Vincent Astor Foundation; and The Scripps Howard Foundation. We also wish to thank Hildy Simmons, Linda L. Gillies, and David Hendin for their assistance.

This book could not have been realized without the kind and generous cooperation of the author, Maya Angelou, and her publisher, Random House, Inc.

We deeply appreciate the contributions of the following suppliers: Cam Steel Die Rule Works Inc. (steel cutting die for display); Domtar Industries (text stock); Federal Paper Board Company, Inc. and Milton Paper Company Inc. (cover stock); Jackson Typesetting (text typesetting); Lancer Graphic Industries, Inc. (cover printing); Martin/Friess Communications (display header); Mergenthaler Container (corrugated display); Offset Paperback Mfrs., Inc., A Bertelsmann Company (text printing and binding); and Stevenson Photo Color Company (cover color separations).

Our thanks to Paul Davis Studio and Claudia Bruno, José Conde, Myrna Davis, Paul Davis, and Jeanine Esposito for their inspired design of the books and their covers. We would also like to thank Barbara A. Mancuso of *The New York Times* Pictures for her help with photo research and selection.

Contents

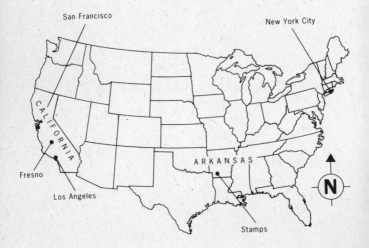

About *Writers' Voices*

"I want to read what others do—what I see people reading in libraries, on the subway, and at home."

Mamie Moore, a literacy student,
Brooklyn, New York

Writers' Voices is our response to Mamie Moore's wish:

the wish to step forward into the reading community,

the wish to have access to new information,

the wish to read to her grandchildren,

the wish to read for the joy of reading.

Note to the Reader

"What we are familiar with, we cease to see. The writer shakes up the familiar scene, and as if by magic, we see a new meaning in it."

Anaïs Nin

Writers' Voices invites you to discover new meaning. One way to discover new meaning is to learn something new. Another is to see in a new way something you already know. Writers touch us by writing about familiar things—love, family, death, for example. Even if the experiences in a book are different from our own, the emotions may be familiar. Our own thoughts and feelings let us interact with the author's story.

Writers' Voices is a series of books. Each book contains unedited selections from one writer's work. We chose the selections because the writers' voices can be clearly heard. Also, they deal with experiences that are interesting to think about and discuss.

If you are a new reader, you may want to have a selection read aloud to you, perhaps more than once. This will free you to enjoy the piece, to hear the language used, and to think about its meaning. Even if you are a more experienced reader, you may enjoy hearing the selection read aloud before reading it silently to yourself.

Each selection is set in a framework to expand your understanding of the selection. The framework includes a chapter that tells about the writer's life. Some authors write about their own lives; other authors write stories from their imagination. You may wonder why an author chose to write what he or she did. Sometimes you can find the answer by knowing about the author's life.

You may also find chapters about the characters, the plot, and when or where the story took place. These will help you begin thinking about the selection. They will also help you understand what may be unfamiliar to you.

We believe that to be a reader, you must be at the center of the reading process. We believe you learn best when you choose what you will read. We encourage you to read *actively*. An active reader does many things—while reading, and before and after reading—that help him or her better understand and enjoy a book. Here are some suggestions of things you can do:

Before Reading
- Read the front and back covers of the book, and look at the cover illustration. Think about what you expect the book to be about, based on this information.
- Think about why you want to read this book.
- Ask yourself what you want to discover, and what questions you hope will be answered.
- Think about how your own experiences and knowledge can help you better understand the book.

During Reading
- Try to stay with the rhythm of the language. If you find any words or sentences you don't understand, keep reading to see if the meaning becomes clear. If it doesn't, go back and reread the difficult part or discuss it with others. If you prefer to wait until you have read the whole story before you reread the difficult part, underline it so it will be easy to find later.
- Put yourself into the story. If you feel left out, ask why. Is it the writing? Is it something else?
- Ask yourself questions as you read. For example: Do I believe this story or this character? Why?

After Reading
- Ask yourself if the story makes you see any of your own experiences in a new way.
- Ask yourself if the story has given you any new information.
- Keep a journal in which you can

write down your thoughts about what you have read, and save new words you have learned.

• Discuss what you have read with others.

Good writing should make you think after you put the book down. Whether you are a beginning reader, a more experienced reader, or a teacher of reading, we encourage you to take time to think about these books and to discuss your thoughts with others.

When you finish a selection, you may want to choose among the questions and suggested activities that follow. They are meant to help you discover more about what you have read and how it relates to you—as a person, as a reader, and as a writer.

When you are finished with the book, we hope you will write to our editors about your reactions. We want to know your thoughts about our books, and what they have meant to you.

About Maya Angelou

Maya Angelou was born on April 4, 1928, in St. Louis, Missouri. Her first name is really Marguerite, but her older brother Bailey used to call her "mya sister." That is how she got the name she uses today.

Maya Angelou's parents were Vivian and Bailey Johnson. They separated when she was three years old, and the two children were sent to live with their grandmother and their Uncle Willie in Stamps, Arkansas.

Annie Henderson, Maya's grandmother, owned a general store in the part of town where blacks lived. The whole family lived in the back of the store, in which the children loved to help.

Maya and her brother Bailey lived there for almost five years. One day their father came and took them to St. Louis, where their mother lived. Maya and Bailey lived with their mother's parents, the Baxters, for about six months. Then they moved in with their mother and her boyfriend, Mr. Freeman. Maya was eight and Bailey was nine.

One day when her mother was at work, Mr. Freeman raped Maya. He was convicted of the crime, but his lawyer got him released before he was sent to prison. Soon after, however, Mr. Freeman was found beaten to death.

Maya felt guilty about her rape and about Mr. Freeman's death. She reacted by becoming silent, but her family did not understand why she refused to talk. They sent Maya and her brother back to her grandmother in Arkansas. It took Maya more than a year to feel like herself again.

During the next years, Maya worked hard at school. After she graduated from eighth grade, her grandmother decided that the children needed to get away from the South and be with their mother. The children moved to San Francisco, California, where their mother now lived.

Maya continued to do well in school, but she was very restless. She decided to become the first black conductor on the San Francisco streetcars. Every day, she went to the office of the streetcar company. Finally, they gave her a job application form to fill in. She wrote that she was 19, even though she was only 15. And she got the job.

When Maya was sixteen, she became pregnant. She did not want to marry the father, whom she did not love. But she wanted the baby. She had the baby soon after graduating from high school. She named him Guy.

Since then, Maya Angelou has done many things. She has been a cook, a cocktail waitress, and a madam. She went on to become a singer and an actress.

In the 1960s, Maya was active in the civil rights movement. At the request of Martin Luther King, Jr., she became the northern coordinator for the Southern Christian Leadership Conference. Also during the 1960s, she lived for four years in Ghana, just after that African country became independent.

Maya Angelou has written five books about her life. She has written books of poetry, movies and plays.

MAYA ANGELOU'S FAMILY TREE

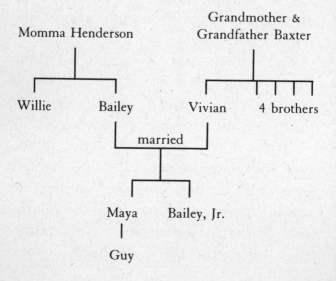

About Joe Louis

This chapter provides a short historical background for the selection.

Joe Louis was born on May 13, 1914, in the mountains of Alabama. He became the most famous black American of his time, the heavyweight champion of the world. He held that title from 1937 to 1949. During his career, he fought 71 fights and lost only 3.

Joe Louis had seven brothers and sisters. He was the next to youngest. His father, Munroe Barrow, was sent to an insane asylum when Joe was two years old. Lillie Barrow, Joe Louis's mother, remarried. Her new husband, Pat Brooks, had eight children of his own.

In 1926, the family moved to Detroit, Michigan, where they lived in a tenement. Joe Louis was not prepared for the Detroit city schools, and was held back.

Joe's stepfather lost his job during the

Depression, so Joe did odd jobs to help the family out. He joined a recreation center to learn to box, because a successful boxer could make good money. In 1933, Joe Louis began boxing as an amateur. He fought 54 fights and won 50 of them. The winner got stamps that could be exchanged for groceries.

In time, Joe Louis came to the attention of John Roxborough, a black who was Detroit's leading numbers operator. When Joe was ready to turn pro, Roxborough and a friend became his managers. They took him to Chicago, Illinois, for training, and Joe had his first professional fight there on July 4, 1934. He won it, and got a prize of $59. He kept on winning fights, and sent most of the money home to his family.

Joe was now ready to break into the big time. Because he was black, his managers had a hard time arranging a major bout. A fight promoter in New York City was starting a new club to compete with Madison Square Garden, and he believed that a fight between Joe Louis and a white boxer would draw big crowds.

The promoter arranged for Joe Louis to fight Primo Carnera, a former heavyweight champion from Italy. The fight was held in Yankee Stadium on June 25, 1935. Joe knocked Carnera out in the sixth round. The next morning, Joe Louis's name was on the front page of all the newspapers. He had made it to the big time.

On June 19, 1936, Joe lost his first professional fight to Max Schmeling, a German. The loss cost him a chance to fight for the heavyweight title. But a chance for the title came a year later, when he faced James J. Braddock at Comiskey Park in Chicago on June 22, 1937. He knocked Braddock out in the eighth round. Joe Louis had become the youngest heavyweight champion ever. He was only 23 years old.

Now that he was heavyweight champion, Joe wanted a rematch with the one man who had defeated him—the German, Max Schmeling. The fight was set for June 22, 1938, in Yankee Stadium. The American people knew that a Nazi movement was growing in Germany and Americans were worried that this would lead to war. When Joe Louis knocked Schmeling out in the first round, the American people—both black and white— cheered because the German had been beaten.

The United States entered World War II in December of 1941, and Joe Louis wanted to help his country. When he fought a title fight against Buddy Baer on January 9, 1942, he gave all his winnings to the Navy Relief Society. The next day, he volunteered for service in the Army. The Army asked him to be an officer, but Joe felt he didn't have enough education. He chose to be a private.

When the war ended, Joe was glad to get back to regular life. He fought Jersey Joe Walcott in 1947 and 1948. They

were difficult fights, and he realized he was getting older. He didn't want to risk losing the heavyweight crown. So on March 1, 1949, Joe Louis retired from boxing.

Over the years, Joe had earned a great deal of money. But he had not been careful with it, and he owed the government a lot of unpaid income taxes. The only way he could earn enough money to pay these taxes was to make a comeback.

Joe Louis fought the current heavyweight champion, Ezzard Charles, on September 27, 1950. Everyone could see that Joe was not the boxer he used to be. He went the distance, but lost the fight on a decision.

On October 26, 1951, Joe fought Rocky Marciano at Madison Square Garden. Marciano, a strong young boxer, knocked Joe out in the eighth round. Everyone, including Joe Louis, knew this had been his last fight.

Over the next years, Joe lived on his reputation, and was helped by the many

friends he had made during his boxing career. He died on April 12, 1981. At his memorial service, Frank Sinatra gave a speech. Sammy Davis, Jr. sang a song. The eulogy was given by the Reverend Jesse Jackson, whose middle name is "Louis," after Joe Louis. Jackson said, "Joe made everybody somebody."

Joe Louis in 1942 (Credit: *The New York Times*)

For biographical information on Joe Louis, we have relied on Chris Mead's *Champion: Joe Louis, Black Hero in White America* (New York, 1985).

About the Selection from
*I Know Why the Caged
Bird Sings*

One of Maya Angelou's many books about her life is *I Know Why the Caged Bird Sings*, which tells about her childhood and early teenage years. This selection, from that book, takes place when Maya is about nine years old. She and her older brother Bailey are living with her grandmother and Uncle Willie in Stamps, Arkansas.

The general store that Maya's grandmother owns is the meeting place of the black people of Stamps. One evening, everyone is in the store to listen to a boxing match on the radio. Joe Louis is one of the boxers.

Perhaps this selection will remind you of a time when you felt proud to be who and what you are. Perhaps it will remind you of a time you shared something important with a group of other people.

Selected from

I Know Why the Caged Bird Sings

The last inch of space was filled, yet
people continued to wedge themselves
along the walls of the Store. Uncle Willie had turned the radio up to its last
notch so that youngsters on the porch
wouldn't miss a word. Women sat on
kitchen chairs, dining-room chairs, stools
and upturned wooden boxes. Small children and babies perched on every lap
available and men leaned on the shelves
or on each other.

The apprehensive mood was shot
through with shafts of gaiety, as a black
sky is streaked with lightning.

"I ain't worried 'bout this fight. Joe's
gonna whip that cracker like it's open
season."

"He gone whip him till that white
boy call him Momma."

At last the talking was finished and

the string-along songs about razor blades were over and the fight began.

"A quick jab to the head." In the Store the crowd grunted. "A left to the head and a right and another left." One of the listeners cackled like a hen and was quieted.

"They're in a clench, Louis is trying to fight his way out."

Some bitter comedian on the porch said, "That white man don't mind hugging that niggah now, I betcha."

"The referee is moving in to break them up, but Louis finally pushed the contender away and it's an uppercut to the chin. The contender is hanging on, now he's backing away. Louis catches him with a short left to the jaw."

A tide of murmuring assent poured out the doors and into the yard.

"Another left and another left. Louis is saving that mighty right. . ." The mutter in the Store had grown into a baby roar and it was pierced by the clang of a bell and the announcer's

"That's the bell for round three, ladies and gentlemen."

As I pushed my way into the Store I wondered if the announcer gave any thought to the fact that he was addressing as "ladies and gentlemen" all the Negroes around the world who sat sweating and praying, glued to their "master's voice."

There were only a few calls for R. C. Colas, Dr. Peppers, and Hire's root beer. The real festivities would begin after the fight. Then even the old Christian ladies who taught their children and tried themselves to practice turning the other cheek would buy soft drinks, and if the Brown Bomber's victory was a particularly bloody one they would order peanut patties and Baby Ruths also.

Bailey and I lay the coins on top of the cash register. Uncle Willie didn't allow us to ring up sales during a fight. It was too noisy and might shake up the atmosphere. When the gong rang for the next round we pushed through the near-sacred quiet to the herd of children outside.

"He's got Louis against the ropes and now it's a left to the body and a right to the ribs. Another right to the body, it looks like it was low ... Yes, ladies and gentlemen, the referee is signaling but the contender keeps raining the blows on Louis. It's another to the body, and it looks like Louis is going down."

My race groaned. It was our people falling. It was another lynching, yet another Black man hanging on a tree. One more woman ambushed and raped. A Black boy whipped and maimed. It was hounds on the trail of a man running through slimy swamps. It was a white woman slapping her maid for being forgetful.

The men in the Store stood away from the walls and at attention. Women greedily clutched the babes on their laps while on the porch the shufflings and smiles, flirtings and pinching of a few minutes before were gone. This might be the end of the world. If Joe lost we were back in slavery and beyond help. It would all be true, the accusations that we were lower types of human beings. Only a little higher than the apes. True that we were stupid and ugly and lazy and dirty and, unlucky and worst of all, that God Himself hated us and ordained us to be hewers of wood and drawers of water, forever and ever, world without end.

We didn't breathe. We didn't hope. We waited.

"He's off the ropes, ladies and gentlemen. He's moving towards the center of the ring." There was no time to be relieved. The worst might still happen.

"And now it looks like Joe is mad. He's caught Carnera with a left hook to the head and a right to the head. It's a left jab to the body and another left to the head. There's a left cross and a right to the head. The contender's right eye is bleeding and he can't seem to keep his block up. Louis is penetrating every block. The referee is moving in, but Louis sends a left to the body and it's the uppercut to the chin and the contender is dropping. He's on the canvas, ladies and gentlemen."

Babies slid to the floor as women stood up and men leaned toward the radio.

"Here's the referee. He's counting. One, two, three, four, five, six, seven ... Is the contender trying to get up again?"

All the men in the store shouted, "NO."

"—eight, nine, ten." There were a few sounds from the audience, but they seemed to be holding themselves in against tremendous pressure.

"The fight is all over, ladies and gentlemen. Let's get the microphone over to the referee ... Here he is. He's got the Brown Bomber's hand, he's holding it up ... Here he is ..."

Then the voice, husky and familiar, came to wash over us—"The winnah, and still heavyweight champeen of the world ... Joe Louis."

Champion of the world. A Black boy.

Some Black mother's son. He was the strongest man in the world. People drank Coca-Colas like ambrosia and ate candy bars like Christmas. Some of the men went behind the Store and poured white lightning in their soft-drink bottles, and a few of the bigger boys followed them. Those who were not chased away came back blowing their breath in front of themselves like proud smokers.

It would take an hour or more before the people would leave the Store and head for home. Those who lived too far had made arrangements to stay in town. It wouldn't do for a Black man and his family to be caught on a lonely country road on a night when Joe Louis had proved that we were the strongest people in the world.

About Segregation

*This chapter provides a short historical
background for the selection.*

In the Civil War, which ended in
1865, the states where there was slavery
were defeated. But blacks were still not
truly free. The southern states then passed
unfair laws called "Black Codes," which
kept blacks from using their new rights.

In 1896, the Supreme Court of the
United States said that blacks had "separate but equal rights." This meant that
it was legal to separate blacks and whites,
as long as there were equal facilities for
each. This decision was used to justify
segregation for many years. Blacks could
not use just any school, restaurant, hotel,
or public restroom, but only those facilities set aside for blacks. Blacks had to sit
at the back of a bus.

Big changes began with World War
II. Just before America entered the war
in 1941, factories in the United States

were busy making guns, tanks, and other
needs of war. But most blacks were still
not finding work.

Even the armed forces were segre-
gated. In 1941, A. Philip Randolph, president of the Brotherhood of Sleeping
Car Porters, began organizing a march
on Washington to protest this discrimination. President Franklin Roosevelt met
with Randolph to see if the march could
be prevented. At the meeting, Roosevelt
agreed to Randolph's demands. He is-
sued an order saying, "There shall be no
discrimination in the employment of
workers in defense industries or government because of race, creed, color, or
national origin." Because of this order,
Randolph called off the march.

Some progress was made during the
war. But black soldiers coming home
from the war found that not much had
changed. Both blacks and whites, however, were more aware of the problems.
And blacks were more militant about
doing something to solve them.

A major step was taken in 1954. The National Association for the Advancement of Colored People (NAACP) challenged the school segregation laws. The Supreme Court heard the case. It was called *Brown vs. Board of Education of Topeka, Kansas.* The Court decided that "separate but equal" had no place in education. The Court said that the very fact that schools were "separate" made them unequal.

Protests developed in many parts of the South. From December of 1955 through December of 1956, blacks boycotted buses in Montgomery, Alabama. The boycott began when a black woman, Rosa Parks, was arrested for refusing to give her seat to a white man. Blacks hoped that if they walked instead of paying fares, the bus company would have to change its segregation policy. Blacks would be able to sit where they wanted. In December of 1956, the Supreme Court said that segregation on buses must stop.

The non-violent resistance of the Montgomery boycott was copied in other parts of the country. Even though the protests were peaceful, demonstrators were often brutally beaten. Blacks, and whites too, were even killed in their support of equal rights. In 1957, a major civil rights bill was passed by Congress.

That same year, nine black children tried to register at an all-white school in Little Rock, Arkansas. The Governor of Arkansas called out the National Guard to keep the black children from entering the school. He was breaking the law. Rioting began, and President Eisenhower sent Federal troops to stop the riots and protect the children. The Governor still refused to obey the law. He closed the school down to prevent its integration.

But the movement for civil rights could not be stopped. Over the next few years, because of the on-going protests by thousands of blacks and whites in the South and North, and because of the 1957 civil rights laws, desegregation took place all over the country.

About the Selection from
The Heart of a Woman

One of Maya Angelou's many books about her life is *The Heart of a Woman*. This selection, from that book, takes place in 1959.

Maya Angelou is living in Los Angeles, California. She decides to move to New York City, where she can work with other black writers.

Guy, Maya's son, is a teenager. Maya worries about him. She thinks a move will be good for both Guy and herself.

Before she leaves California, she wants to visit her mother, Vivian Baxter Jackson, who lives in San Francisco. Maya's mother suggests that they meet at a hotel in Fresno, California. The hotel has just been desegregated.

Perhaps this selection will make you think about a big decision, such as moving, that you have made. Perhaps it will make you consider your own feelings about prejudice and discrimination.

Selected from

The Heart of a Woman

I called my mother and she answered after the first ring.

"Hello?"

"Lady?"

"Oh hello, baby." She spoke as crisply as a white woman.

I said, "I'd like to see you. I'm going to move to New York and I don't know when I'll come back to California. Maybe we could meet somewhere and spend a couple of days together. I could drive north, part of the way—"

She didn't pause. "Of course, we can meet, of course, I want to see you, baby." Six feet tall, with a fourteen-year-old son, and I was still called baby. "How about Fresno? That's halfway. We could stay at that hotel. I know you read about it."

"Yes. But not if there's going to be trouble. I just want to be with you."

"Trouble? Trouble?" The familiar

knife edge had slipped into her voice. "But, baby, you know that's my middle name. Anyway, the law says that hotel has to accept Negro guests. I'll swear before God and five other responsible men that my daughter and I are Negroes. After that, if they refuse us, well . . ."—she laughed hopefully and high-pitched—"well, we'll have a board to fit their butts."

That part of the conversation was finished. Vivian Baxter sensed the possibility of confrontation and there would be no chance of talking her out of it. I realized too late that I should simply have taken the Southern Pacific train from Los Angeles to San Francisco and spent the two days in her Fulton Street house, then returned to pack for my continental move.

Her voice softened again as she relayed family gossip and set a date for our meeting in the middle of the state.

• • •

In 1959, Fresno was a middling town with palm trees and a decidedly Southern accent. Most of its white inhabitants seemed to be descendants of Steinbeck's Joads, and its black citizens were farm hands who had simply exchanged the dirt roads of Arkansas and Mississippi for the dusty streets of central California.

I parked my old Chrysler on a side street, and taking my overnight case, walked around the corner to the Desert Hotel. My mother had suggested that we meet at three, which meant that she planned to arrive at two.

The hotel lobby had been decorated with welcome banners for a visiting sales convention. Large florid men mingled and laughed with portly women under low-hanging chandeliers.

My entrance stopped all action. Every head turned to see, every eye blazed, first with doubt, then fury. I wanted to run back to my car, race to Los Angeles, back to the postered walls of my house. I straightened my back and forced my face into indifference and walked to the registration desk. The clock above said two forty-five. "Good afternoon. Where is the bar?" A round-faced young man dropped his eyes and pointed behind me.

"Thank you."

The crowd made an aisle and I walked through the silence, knowing that before I reached the lounge door, a knife could be slipped in my back or a rope lassoed around my neck.

My mother sat at the bar wearing her Dobbs hat and tan suede suit. I set my case down inside the door and joined her.

"Hi, baby," her smile was a crescent of white. "You're a little early." She knew I would be. "Jim?" And I knew she'd already have the bartender's name and his attention. The man grinned for her.

"Jim, this is my baby. She's pretty, isn't she?"

Jim nodded, never taking his eyes away

from Mother. She leaned over and kissed me on the lips.

"Give her a Scotch and water and another little taste for yourself."

She caught him as he started to hesitate. "Don't refuse, Jim. No man can walk on one leg." She smiled, and he turned to prepare the drinks.

"Baby, you're looking good. How was the drive? Still got that old Chrysler? Did you see those people in the lobby? They're so ugly they make you stop and think. How's Guy? Why are you going to New York? Is he happy about the move?"

Jim set my drink down and lifted his in a toast.

Mother picked up her drink. "Here's looking at you, Jim." And to me. "Here's a go, baby." She smiled and I saw again that she was the most beautiful woman I had ever seen.

"Thanks, Mother."

She took my hands, put them together and rubbed them.

"You are cold. Hot as it is, your hands are freezing. Are you all right?"

Nothing frightened my mother except thunder and lightning. I couldn't tell her that at thirty-one years old, the whites in the lobby had scared me silly.

"Just fine, Mother. I guess it's the air conditioning."

She accepted the lie.

"Well, let's drink up and go to our room. I've got some talk for you."

She picked up the bills from the bar, counted them and pulled out two singles.

"What time do you come on, Jim?"

The bartender turned and grinned. "I open up. At eleven every morning."

"Then, I'll break your luck for you. Scotch and water, remember. At eleven. This is for you."

"Oh, you don't have to do that."

Mother was off the stool. "I know. That's why it's easy. See you in the morning."

I picked up my suitcase, followed her out of the dark bar into the noisy lobby.

Again, the buzz of conversation dimin-
ished, but Mother never noticed. She
switched through the crowd, up to the
desk.

"Mrs. Vivian Baxter Jackson and
daughter. You have our reservation." My
mother had married a few times, but
she loved her maiden name. Married or
not, she often identified herself as Vivian Baxter.

It was a statement. "And please call
the bellboy. My bag is in my car. Here
are the keys. Set your bag down here,
baby." Back to the registration clerk.
"And tell him to bring my daughter's
case to our room." The clerk slowly
pushed a form across the counter. Mother
opened her purse, took out her gold
Sheaffer and signed us in.

"The key, please." Again using slow
motion, the clerk slid the key to Mother.

"Two ten. Second floor. Thank you.
Come on, baby." The hotel's color bar
had been lifted only a month earlier, yet
she acted as if she had been a guest

there for years. There was a winding staircase to the right of the desk and a small group of open-mouthed conventioneers standing by the elevator.

I said, "Let's take the stairs, Mother."

She said, "We're taking the elevator," and pushed the "up" button. The waiting people looked at us as if our very presence had stripped everything of value from their lives.

When we got out of the elevator, mother took a moment, then turned and walked left to 210. She unlocked the door and when we entered, she threw her purse on the bed and walked to the window.

"Sit down, baby. I'm going to tell you something you must never forget."

I sat on the first chair as she opened the drapes. The sunlight framed her figure, and her face was indistinct.

"Animals can sense fear. They feel it. Well, you know that human beings are animals, too. Never, never let a person know you're frightened. And a group of them ... absolutely never. Fear brings out the worst thing in everybody. Now, in that lobby you were as scared as a rabbit. I knew it and all those white folks knew it. If I hadn't been there, they might have turned into a mob. But something about me told them, if they mess with either of us, they'd better start looking for some new asses, 'cause I'd blow away what their mammas gave them."

She laughed like a young girl. "Look in my purse." I opened her purse.

"The Desert Hotel better be ready for integration, 'cause if it's not, I'm ready for the Desert Hotel."

Under her wallet, half hidden by her cosmetic case, lay a dark-blue German Luger.

"Room service? This is two ten. I'd like a pitcher of ice, two glasses, and a bottle of Teachers Scotch. Thank you."

The bellboy had brought our bags, and we had showered and changed.

"We'll have a cocktail and go down

for dinner. But now, let's talk. Why New York? You were there in '52 and had to be sent home. What makes you think it has changed?"

"I met a writer, John Killens. I told him I wanted to write and he invited me to New York."

"He's colored, isn't he?" Since my first marriage to a Greek had dissolved, Mother had been hoping for a black son-in-law.

"He's married, Mother. It's not like that."

"That's terrible. First ninety-nine married men out of a hundred never divorce their wives for their girl friends, and the one that does will probably divorce the new wife for a newer girl friend."

"But really, it's not that way. I've met his wife and children. I'll go to New York, stay with them for a couple of weeks, get an apartment and send for Guy."

"And where will he stay for two

weeks? Not alone in that big house. He's only fourteen."

She would explode if I told her I planned for him to stay with the man I was leaving. Vivian Baxter had survived by being healthily suspicious. She would never trust a rejected lover to treat her grandson fairly.

"I've made arrangements with a friend. And after all, it's only two weeks."

We both knew that she had left me and my brother for ten years to be raised by our paternal grandmother. We looked at each other and she spoke first.

"You're right. It is only two weeks. Well, let me tell you about me. I'm going to sea."

"To see. See what?"

"I'm going to become a merchant marine."

I had never heard of a female merchant seaman.

"A member of the Marine Cooks and Stewards Union."

"Why?" Disbelief raised my voice.

"Why?" She was a surgical nurse, a realtor, had a barber's license and owned a hotel. Why did she want to go to sea and live the rough unglamorous life of a seaman?

"Because they told me Negro women couldn't get in the union. You know what I told them?"

I shook my head, although I nearly knew.

"I told them, 'You want to bet?' I'll put my foot in that door up to my hip until women of every color can walk over my foot, get in that union, get aboard a ship and go to sea." There was a knock at the door. "Come in."

A uniformed black man opened the door and halted in surprise at seeing us.

"Good evening. Just put the tray over there. Thank you."

The bellboy deposited the tray and turned.

"Good evening, you all surprised me. Sure did. Didn't expect to see you. Sure didn't."

Mother walked toward him holding money in her hand.

"Who did you expect? Queen Victoria?"

"No. No, ma'am. I mean ... Our people ... in here ... It's kinda new seeing us ... and everything."

"This is for you." She gave him the tip. "We are just ordinary guests in the hotel. Thank you and good night." She opened the door and waited. When he walked out mumbling good night, she closed the door with finality.

"Mom, you were almost rude."

"Well, baby, I figure like this. He's colored and I'm colored, but we are not cousins. Let's have a drink." She smiled.

During the next two days, Mother showed me off to some old card-playing friends she had known twenty years earlier.

"This is my baby. She's been to Egypt, all around Milan, Italy, and Spain and Yugoslavia. She's a singer and dancer, you know." When her friends were satisfactorily impressed with my accomplishments, Mother made certain of their wonder by adding, "Of course, I'll be shipping out myself in a few days."

We hugged in the empty lobby of the Desert Hotel; the convention had ended the day before our departure.

"Take care of yourself. Take care of your son, and remember New York City is just like Fresno. Just more of the same people in bigger buildings. Black folks can't change because white folks won't change. Ask for what you want and be prepared to pay for what you get." She kissed me and her voice softened to a whisper. "Let me leave first, baby. I hate to see the back of someone I love."

We embraced again and I watched her walk, hips swaying, into the bright street.

Your Thoughts about the Selections
from *I Know Why the Caged Bird Sings*
and *The Heart of a Woman*

1. What did you think of the selections from *I Know Why the Caged Bird Sings* and *The Heart of a Woman*? Did you like them? Why?

2. Are there ways that the events or people in the selections became important or special to you? Write or discuss why.

3. What parts of the selections were the most interesting? Why?

4. Were the selections what you expected they would be? Did they answer the questions you had before you began reading or listening? In what way did they?

5. Was there anything new or surprising to you in the selections? What?

QUESTIONS FOR THE READER

Thinking about the Story

1. Describe the people in the selection from *I Know Why the Caged Bird Sings* and in the selection from *The Heart of a Woman*. Which do you think are the most important in each selection? Why?

2. What do you think was the most important thing Maya Angelou wanted to say in each selection?

3. What have you learned about Maya Angelou from reading each selection? If you read the Joe Louis fight selection, why do you think the fight was important to the people in the store? Why do you think it was important to Maya Angelou? Find some examples to support your opinion. If you read the selection about Maya and her mother, what do you think their relationship is? Find some examples to support your opinion.

4. As you were listening or reading, what were your thoughts as the story unfolded?

5. Were any parts of the selections difficult to understand? If so, you may want to read or listen to them again. You might think about why they were difficult.

QUESTIONS FOR THE READER

Thinking about the Writing

1. How did Maya Angelou help you see, hear, and feel what happened in each selection? Find the words, phrases, or sentences that you think did this best.

2. Writers think very carefully about their stories' settings, characters, and events. In writing each selection, which of these things do you think Maya Angelou felt was most important? Find the parts of the story that support your opinion.

3. Which character in each selection was most interesting to you? How did Maya Angelou help you learn about this person? Find the places in each selection where you learned the most about this person.

4. In each selection, Maya Angelou uses dialogue. Dialogue can make a story stronger and more alive. Pick out some dialogue that you feel is strong, and explain how it helps the story.

5. The selections are seen through Maya Angelou's eyes. She uses the words "I" and "me." How would the writing be different if the story was told from another character's point of view (such as Bailey's or her mother's), or from your own point of view?

6. *If you read the Joe Louis fight selection, please answer this question.* When we read about the fight, we experience it as if we were there ourselves. How does Maya Angelou bring us into this experience? Find the places where you feel most involved with the story.

7. *If you read the selection about Maya Angelou and her mother, please answer this question.* Maya Angelou's mother is a very strong person. Which parts of the selection gave you the clearest impression of the kind of person she is?

Activities

1. Were there any words that were difficult for you in the selection from *I Know Why the Caged Bird Sings* and the selection from *The Heart of a Woman*? Go back to these words and try to figure out their meanings. Discuss what you think each word means, and why you made that guess.

2. Are there any words new to you in each selection that you would like to remember? Discuss with your teacher or another student how you are going to remember each word. You could put them on file cards, or write them in your journal, or create a personal dictionary. Be sure to use each word in a sentence of your own.

3. How did you help yourself understand each selection? Did you ask yourself questions? What were they? Discuss these questions with other people who have read the same selection, or write about them in your journal.

4. Talking with other people about what you have read can increase your understanding of it. Discussion can help you organize your thoughts, get new ideas, and rethink your original ideas. Discuss your thoughts about each selection with someone else who has read it. Find out if your opinions are the same or different. See if your thoughts change as a result of this discussion.

5. If you like a selection, you might want to encourage someone else to read it. You could write a book review, or a letter to a friend you think might be interested in reading the book.

6. Sometimes organizing information in a visual way can help you better understand or remember it. Look at Maya Angelou's family tree. You might want to make a family tree of your own.

7. If you could talk to Maya Angelou, what questions would you ask about her writing? You might want to write the questions in your journal.

8. Is there something you kept thinking about after reading each selection? What? Write about why it is meaningful to you.

If you read the Joe Louis fight selection, please consider the following activities:

9. Did the selection give you any ideas for your own writing? You might want to write about:

   • an experience you shared with a group of people, like the people in the store.
   • a particular moment that made you proud to be who you are.
   • an exciting event you heard on the radio or saw on television.

10. Think about your own life when you were growing up, and what the world was like for you. You might want to write about some of your memories. Perhaps you will want to share them with someone else.

11. It was very important to the blacks in the store that Joe Louis win this fight. They felt he fought for all of them. Can you think of any other men or women—in the past and in the present—who are important to people in this way? If you can, you may wish to write about how and why they are important.

If you read the selection about Maya Angelou and her mother, please consider the following activities:

12. Did reading the selection give you any ideas for your own writing? You might want to write about:

    • your own relationship with a parent.
    • a big decision, such as moving, that you have made.
    • your thoughts about civil rights.

13. Think about a strong person you have known who has influenced you in some way. Why was this person important to you? You might want to write about this person, or write a letter to him or her.

14. This selection is about Maya Angelou, her mother, and her son. Think about three generations of your own family, or of a family you know. How do the relationships compare to the relationships in the selection?